The CANNABIS CRAZE

A PRACTICAL GUIDE for Parents and Teens

Marc Aronoff

Illustrated by Earl Cavanah

PORTER HOUSE

Porter House
33 Saint Ann's Ave
Lenox, MA 01240

The publisher is not responsible for websites
(or their content) that are not owned by the publisher.

First Edition: October, 2014
Second Edition: 2016
Third Edition: 2019

Summary: Self-improvement, harm reduction, and
guidance on use of marijuana among teens.

ISBN: 978-1-63041-020-9 Paperback
ISBN: 978-1-63041-143-5 e-Book
ISBN: 978-1-63041-488-7 Audiobook

Library of Congress Catalog Card Number: 20-14909616

Printed in the United States of America

CONTENTS

DON'T READ THIS... 9

THE BEGINNING 13

HELLO 15

WHY START?.. 19

WHAT IS IN MARIJUANA? 23

CRAZY TEEN YEARS.. 25

CURIOUS 29

FIRST TIME... 31

WHAT DOES GETTING HIGH FEEL LIKE? 35

I LIKE IT!.. 37

A LITTLE REALITY... 39

SMOKING WITH OTHERS 43

THE SOMETIMES SMOKER 45

THE EVERYDAY SMOKER 47

BUYING POT 49

HIDING YOUR FIRST "DIME"... 51

THE DRAMA 54

SECRETS AND LIES 56

I HATE YOU... 60

COMMUNICATION 62

PARENT(S) 64

THE GOOD-ENOUGH PARENT 68

EXTREME PARENTS.. 72

BOUNDARIES 74

POT-SMOKING PARENTS 76

SAFE... 78

SCHOOL.. 80

COLLEGE 82

KNOWING YOURSELF 84

TOO MUCH 86

HEALTH... 88

ADDICTION.. 92

POT VS. ALCOHOL 96

POLICE.. 99

STRESS 101

IS POT MEDICINE? 105

THE STATE OF MODERN HERB 107

POLITICS 109

THE NEXT LEVEL 111

SUCCESS 113

CREATIVITY 115

A JOB-JOB 117

LOVE... 119

THE TRUE YOU.. 121

JUST ONE PUFF.. 123

WORDS, WORDS, WORDS 125

STRENGTH IS ALSO VULNERABILITY 127

REINVENT YOURSELF 129

GOOD-BYE 131

ABOUT THE AUTHOR 135

ABOUT THE ILLUSTRATOR.. 137

Visit us on the web at
www.thecannabiscraze.com

DON'T READ THIS

Now that I have your attention, let me tell you a little story. While living in Europe working as a professional dancer, I traveled extensively and had the chance to interact with many different cultures. Once, after a performance in Berlin, we attended an "underground" music event in an abandoned factory. During the intermission a German musician was rolling a joint with tobacco and hash sprinkled together and one of the dancers in our troupe suggested leaving the tobacco out. The joint roller commented, "What? You want only the hashish?"

"Yes," said the American sincerely. "Why add tobacco?"

Then the German fellow paused and looked up. "You know," he said, "we Germans just want to relax and be social when we smoke pot. You Americans want to get f—up! You just want to get f—up!"

He had a point.

With marijuana and alcohol, it appears many young Americans are only interested in consuming to excess. Young Europeans in general begin drinking legally at age sixteen because, I believe, they have a sense of maturity, balance, and common sense about "catching a buzz." It is not about getting f—up. It is about being smart, knowing your limits, and enjoying the moment. That is balance.

I understand the topic this book addresses is controversial and not everyone is supportive of an open discussion. In the United States, marijuana is illegal for anyone under age twenty-one, and that will likely never change. However, just as there are sex education classes for teens (who are not supposed to be engaging in sex), I believe education is appropriate for the millions of teens who are not supposed to be smoking pot...but will anyway.

In working with teens as a licensed counselor over the last twenty years, I have seen many succeed and change shape as they moved through the often difficult years of adolescence. I have also seen many struggle to find that next step that moves them from problem child to thriving young adult. Some teens simply have an easier time with the emotions, burdens, and challenges of adolescence, and some truly struggle. The reasons are many, from mental health and genetics to parenting style and coping skills. I am a cognitive-behavioral counselor and primarily work within a framework that teaches, smart choices reduce suffering.

In writing this book, it is my intent to explore pertinent issues posed to me over the years by teens who smoke marijuana. I hope this will lead to the possibility of teens and parents discussing marijuana in a healthy and respectful manner. Some of you may think pot is no big deal. Others may think the drug is horrible and to be forbidden at all costs. I try and walk a middle path. Whatever your personal opinion on the subject, the availability and perceived acceptance of marijuana has never been greater than today. This is true for both adults and teens. My hope is this book will help deepen a mature discussion on the subject.

THE BEGINNING

HELLO

We were parked in a parking garage, top floor, with a view of the distant mountains. All of us, Jimmy, Ronnie, and me, were sixteen years old. The sun was setting, and the sky was glowing red and purple and orange as we passed the joint around on a hot summer night. Suddenly, a car pulled up next to us, and Jimmy's mom got out. We were busted! But, Jimmy's mom did not freak out. She asked us all to get out of the car and had a talk with us right there on the parking garage. She was disappointed in all of us, but somehow let us know she really cared. I remember thinking, what a cool mom. Then she went home.

Marijuana is on America's mind. According to a recent study by the Partnership at Drugfree.org, one in ten American teens smoke marijuana at least twenty or more times per month. That means over two million teens smoke pot regularly, many every day. Though marijuana remains illegal for anyone under the age of twenty-one, the reality is that millions of American teens will try marijuana this year. As of this edition, medical marijuana is legal in over 30 states. Numerous states have legalized marijuana for recreational use and several other states have relaxed marijuana drug laws. Internationally, the countries of Uruguay and Canada have legalized marijuana. Comparatively, the harshest laws for marijuana possession are in places like Japan, Indonesia, and most Arab countries where laws for possession are strict and those caught selling the drug may be sentenced to death.

This book is not about promoting or discouraging the smoking of marijuana. This is about the reality of smoking pot and *harm reduction*. The idea for writing the book came about from a series of conversations with a colleague. He is a licensed counselor for at-risk youth, and many of his teen patients smoke pot. We discussed the need for young people who smoke pot to be smart about it. Smart does not mean book smart. Smart means knowing how to be successful, thrive, and create a good life in the present, which leads to the future.

In the end, *Cannabis Craze* is a young person's survival guidebook to something millions of Americans do: smoke weed. Knowing how to *smoke smart* is essential for maintaining a balanced life, in which you feel good about your personal choices and accomplishments. And, if you have not noticed, balance is essential to survival. Without it, people, get sick. With balance, which takes practice, life's journey is simply more enjoyable. This balance will ideally allow you to blossom as an individual and pursue your dreams.

Does this thing come with operating instructions? Actually, yes. Read on.

WHY START?

There are many reasons young people start smoking pot, but some of the most important reasons are:

1. Relaxing and escaping from the pressures of life.
2. Belonging to a community and making friendships.
3. Developing a personal identity.
4. Peer pressure.

For the most part, teens are on their own when it comes to smoking pot. Many parents will say and see nothing, unless there is a problem. Maybe your parents have a little marijuana chat with you, but if you are doing well with school, home, and friends, there is often less worry from Mom or Dad. That's fine. Teens figure things out as they go along.

People ask, "Aren't adolescent pot smokers generally unproductive, lazy, and goofy, messing up their short-term memory, among other brain functions?" Yes. And no. Science is still figuring out the long-term effects of smoking pot. A big concern is how a beginner handles smoking pot. The reality is that there are young people who are *smart* about smoking (and by smart, I mean having common sense and discipline). *How* you smoke pot (if you smoke pot) is important. Some young people make a mess of smoking pot and do poorly at school. Some young people do fine.

In a groundbreaking study (March 2014) Peggy van der Pol of the Trimbos Institute of the Netherlands Institute of Mental Health and Addiction, determined that *how* pot is smoked affects addiction risk.

Because some people will thrive and get ahead in life, while occasionally smoking pot, and others will not, knowing how to smoke smart is essential. *How* you smoke pot means how often, where, and when.

REFLECTION: If you smoke pot, why did you start?

Knowledge is power.

WHAT IS IN MARIJUANA?

Marijuana is a plant that gets you *high* when inhaled or eaten because of a group of 85 active compounds known as Cannabinoids. THC, tetrahydrocannabinol and Cannabidiol or CBD are the two primary chemicals that create feelings of well being and relaxation. The higher the percentage of THC and CBD in marijuana the stronger it is. Stronger pot, however, does not mean a better feeling. There is such a thing as too strong and too much *for you*. Today's pot is stronger than yesterday's, so you don't need as much to get high. There are three "types" or strains of marijuana that are generally available: Indica, Sativa, and Hybrids. Though they will effect each unique person differently, Indica, is often relaxing, Sativa, uplifting, and the hybrid's a mix. In the seventies and eighties, pot had 3–5 percent THC. Today high-end pot is over 30 percent THC. (More on this later).

Marijuana is generally smoked. It can also be vaporized as well as eaten in brownies, cookies, and baked goods. Medical marijuana is also available in oils, tinctures, lozenges, and edibles. I'd like to mention, however, there are some particular risks with *edibles* because they give a more intense, longer-lasting, and sometimes hallucinogenic high. This can be extreme and dangerous. Edibles take longer to take effect and if too much is eaten—not good.

Hemp is a marijuana plant without the THC. Even though it looks like marijuana, it will not get you high, and it is not sold to be smoked. However, it is sold commercially and is an incredible plant with many uses, like making blue jeans, beer, and fuel.

REFLECTION: Where were you the first time you saw or smelled pot?

Today's pot is stronger than yesterdays.

CRAZY TEEN YEARS

When do most people begin smoking pot?
Adolescence.

From about the age of thirteen to nineteen, teens reveal a unique mix of opinion, confusion, experimentation, self-expression, challenging authority, and hormonal energy—all the stuff that makes for human evolution and progress. And every young person is different. Some mature faster than others. Some teens are out of control and feel overwhelmed, some moody and angry, some quiet and shy, some athletic, some smart and sassy, some anxious, some brilliant, some depressed, some nerdy; the list goes on, yet all come together by testing limits and experimenting with the world of becoming an adult.

Science knows the prefrontal cortex of the brain—which is the part in charge of understanding consequences and making smart choices for the future—is not fully developed until about age twenty-four. That means that during adolescence, as the brain develops, the average young person does not think much about consequences, because that part of the brain is developing. Adolescents are prone to say and do things in the moment, without much thought. If you add alcohol or drugs to that teen brain, there is an increased chance for senseless, harmful behavior.

So a little help from a trusted adviser or good book may be in order at this time of life. The resolution of adolescence evolves over time. Working out the answers to the universal questions: Who am I? What do I care about? takes patience. There is no getting around adolescence. Add to adolescence thinking about or trying pot, and you have the average American teen.

REFLECTION: What is the hardest thing for you at this time in your life?

Making good choices takes practice.

CURIOUS

There is a good chance most teens in this country will be faced with the choice to smoke marijuana. If you are curious about it, that is normal. Marijuana is around a majority of American high schools and cities; that is a reality.

When, how, or why pot might cross your path is less essential than the fact that it will; a day will likely come, sometime, somewhere, and there it is—marijuana, weed, pot, buddha, herb, dope, ganja, boom, Mary Jane, gangster, chronic, cannabis. Whatever you call it, that smell cannot be mistaken. Then it is your choice to try pot or not.

Maybe your friends are trying pot and talking about it. Maybe they like it. Maybe they don't. Hopefully, your parents (or parent) have said something to you about pot, expressing their opinion—not an opinion they shove down your throat, but a caring, respectful opinion. Hopefully, your parents communicate about how to handle peer pressure or being true to yourself, about how to handle drugs, sex, and parties, or whatever might be happening. Yes, parents should say a few words, short and sweet, state an opinion, share a philosophy; that is what being a parent involves. Being a curious teen is normal. Not trying pot, for whatever reason, is normal also.

REFLECTION: If you do not smoke pot, what are your reasons?

Curiosity is normal.

FIRST TIME

Whether you are smoking from a bowl, joint, spliff, apple, bong, vape, or one of the many ways to smoke, you will probably not get high the first time. This is true for many first-timers, but not all. Some people get blasted the first time they try pot. But, often nothing happens until at least the second or third time.

The reason that you don't get high the first time you smoke pot is because when you are first introduced to THC, your body is unfamiliar with the ingredient in pot that gets you high. But after the second or even third time, your body will know what to do with the THC and you will feel an intense high that is often called "the highest you will ever be."

The first high from pot can be intense. Hopefully, you are hanging out with a few cool people or friends you trust. You should feel comfortable, though being a little nervous is normal. Smoking for the first time, many teens just take one or two puffs, hold them in for a few seconds, and exhale. It can take up to twenty minutes to feel anything.

So after you smoke the first time, you may be around a bunch of people who are stoned, and if you are not, that can be annoying because they may be acting silly. The average first timer attempts two to four times before feeling anything. After your first high, you will then usually feel something after smoking weed anywhere from two to fifteen minutes. The longer you delay beginning smoking pot, the less likely you are to have problems with pot later on. If you start smoking before the age of thirteen, you have a 75 percent chance of becoming a problem pot smoker later on. (A *problem* pot smoker is someone who ends up becoming addicted). Starting after age fifteen reduces the chance of problems. People who start at age twenty-one or older have a 10 percent chance of becoming a problem smoker.

REFLECTION: If you smoke pot, how many times did it take to feel anything?

Your first hit and you feel....well...nothing!

WHAT DOES GETTING
HIGH FEEL LIKE?

While the effects of smoking pot vary from person to person, most people experience:

- Feeling chilled out, relaxed, silly, and happy.
- Feeling hungry, known as "getting the munchies."
- Feeling more aware of sensations—music sounds better, and colors are more vivid.
- Ideas flow in a stream of creative thought and in sight.

Feeling relaxed or silly is common for most beginners who smoke pot. However, your current mood and personality as well as where you are and who you are with will also affect your high. If you are already extremely worried or anxious, you may become more worried or anxious after smoking pot. Some first timers who smoke pot may become paranoid and do not feel good. Some people may feel tired or sleepy after smoking pot and feel it *does nothing* for them. Pot is not for everyone. In particular, if you have severe mental illness, pot can make your life and problems worse. However, many people feel good after getting high.

The feelings of being high usually do not last long. Within a few hours the feeling wears off, depending on the potency of the pot. However, traces of pot stay in your body for several weeks, and subtle effects can last a few days, like feeling spacy, tired, or lazy. This is a good reason not to smoke every day.

REFLECTION: If you tried pot, what happened the first time?

Who you're with effects your mood.

I LIKE IT!

Okay, you tried smoking pot a few times, and you finally felt that high people talk about. What did your first high feel like for you? Relaxed, happy, silly, creative, talkative, spiritual, sleepy, paranoid, scary, lazy, active? Did you feel safe? Where were you? Who was with you?

When you get to the "I like it and want to do it again" phase, it is all the more important to smoke smart. Some teen pot smokers smoke just the right amount at the right time and do not get in trouble. Some young people make a mess of smoking pot and do not do well with parents, school, or responsibilities.

For many young people, being responsible (doing what you say you will do, being where you need to be on time, etc.), is a challenge. Yet, some adolescents have little problem with being responsible. No matter where you are in your maturity, you are always in charge of your choices. If you try pot, it is essential to be smart about it.

REFLECTION: If you like smoking pot, what about it do you like?

It's your choice.

A LITTLE REALITY

The people who most frequently die from the most-abused drugs—street and pharmaceutical opiates—are white, middle-aged adults.

There are many educated and scientific facts about smoking pot in adolescence. (www.drugabuse.gov is an excellent resource). However, one myth I would like to clarify is that marijuana statistically leads to harder drugs. Numerous research projects over the last fifteen years have debunked the idea of pot as a gateway drug. In a report commissioned by Congress to look at the possible dangers of medical marijuana, the Institute of Medicine of the National Academy of Sciences wrote:

There is no conclusive evidence that the drug effects of marijuana are causally linked to the subsequent abuse of other illicit drugs.

True, some young people will start with pot and go on to harder drugs. There are always exceptions. Still, most teens who try pot will not go on to anything harder except college, and they can be as successful as someone who does not smoke pot. The reason most teens do not go on (and become addicted) to harder drugs is because they have no interest in harder drugs. Research indicates that someone who goes on to harder drugs will do so with or without marijuana. Marijuana is the first drug teens try, because it is so readily available.

According to the Center on Juvenile and Criminal Justice, the state of California voted for a decriminalization of smoking or being in possession of small amounts of marijuana. Now there is a small sanction if you are caught smoking marijuana in California, and the punishment is rarely enforced. Are teens going crazy? No. Crime, hard-drug arrests, and school dropout rates actually went down to record lows among California youth. Meanwhile, California's drug-abuse death rate is now below the national average, after many years above. Is it possible that California teens are being smart about how they smoke pot?

What all this means is that you need to know yourself. Are you the kid who will go on to harder drugs, with or without marijuana? Are you the kid who does not know his or her limit and will get into trouble? Do you have an addictive personality? What does it mean to know yourself? If you smoke pot, where do you have to be afterward? Do you ever ask, "Is this a *good* time to smoke pot?" Are you smoking on the way to school? Is this what you truly want to do? Are you being smart about it?

The philosopher Socrates said, "Know thyself." To know yourself means challenging your assumptions and actions and making corrections where needed. That is also called "self-knowledge." Smart teens who are experimenting with smoking pot do so only when they have no responsibilities at home or school.

REFLECTION: Is it possible to be smart about smoking pot?

No thanks.

SMOKING WITH OTHERS

Some young people smoke by themselves. But getting high alone can lead to other problems, including not learning how to socialize, not gaining confidence in being yourself, or not learning how to be accepted by others. Smoking alone can encourage isolation and lead to low self-esteem. There is a saying you are only as healthy as the friends you keep.

Some teens smoke with others and cultivate a feeling of community and feedback. If you smoke, hopefully you are with some mellow friends, and there is nothing wild going on around you, such as crazy drinking or hard drugs. Keep to a few friends or people you trust. Stay away from anyone who is extreme, pushy, manipulating, or forcing you to do anything you don't want to do. Do your best to choose a good group of people. For example, the wrong crowd is mixing alcohol, hard drugs, and driving.

REFLECTION: Do you smoke pot more often by yourself or with others?

Try to smoke with someone you trust.

THE SOMETIMES SMOKER

If you smoke once in a while, you are the *sometimes* smoker, aka the *recreational* smoker.

Once in a while means: a few times a month, or maybe on *some* weekends or *sometimes* after school, or at the *occasional* gathering in the park, but not every day.

For the sometimes or recreational pot smoker, pot is *not* the number one thing in life. Pot is not a priority. If pot is around and the time is right (safe, no school, etc.), sometimes pot smokers may have a puff. But they are smart because they always have a sense of doing other things, activities, and events, without pot. Smart sometimes smokers are more likely to handle smoking marijuana responsibly.

If pot is getting in the way of your personal measures of success, you may be more than a sometimes smoker. Measures of success for a teen may include feeling good about yourself and others, having a few good friends, doing well in school or work, being in balance with sleep and food, and having other interests and hobbies that help keep you happy.

REFLECTION: Where and when do you smoke?

It's been a while.

THE EVERYDAY SMOKER

There will always be those young people who will smoke pot anytime and anywhere they can. They are known as "the stoners." Sometimes they are called "deadbeat stoners" if they are in a rut and get nothing done. In fact, stoners are in high schools all over the world. Everyday smokers take more risks and increase the possibility of getting themselves in trouble with parents or the law, as well as messing up school grades and future prospects (remember brain development!).

Some everyday smokers are extremely intelligent and do well in life and work. Some smokers are a mix of sometimes and everyday, but most everyday smokers will likely not do as well as they could if they smoked less. One way to control smoking pot is using your awareness and willpower to smoke less.

Everyday smoking can quickly become a problem when it starts to interfere with your personal measures of success. What are some measures of success? Same as the sometimes smoker—good grades, good friends, decent attitude, and then off to college. Getting it right means making mistakes and then adjusting as needed; it means you have some good days and some not so good. If you feel your mood is always awful, and you cannot control your feelings, you may need some extra help from a counselor.

REFLECTION: How often do you smoke pot?

Know when it's time to stop.

BUYING POT

The cost of marijuana depends on the potency and quality, with the strongest pot being the most expensive.

Parents often wonder where teens get their pot. Truth is, pot is available, somehow, most everywhere. Many teens have a tight circle of friends and only buy pot from someone they trust. Usually, someone knows someone who can get some. Maybe it is an older brother or sister. Hopefully, it is not your parents buying it for you. More on that later.

Most teens know better than to buy pot from a complete stranger. They usually know the person and have an introduction. Sometimes in these situations you may be offered something other than pot. I strongly suggest saying no thanks. Simple as that. If you begin experimenting with ecstasy, crack, downers, speed, meth, opiates, or anything other than pot, even if it is "recreational," your personal risks for failure increase.

Be smart, and please stay away from *anything* harder than pot.

REFLECTION: Where do you buy pot?

Smoke? Smoke?

HIDING YOUR FIRST "DIME"

For most teens, the practice of hiding pot hiding pot and keeping it secret from their parents is a common. However, this is not true for all teens. If parents and teens have the kind of relationship where it is safe to communicate about difficult subjects, well, kids will tell their parents when they have tried pot. Parents have a right to know you have tried it or are considering smoking—and "good" communication is the first step. I will define good in this case as a relationship between teens and parents based in deep listening and thoughtful responses. Some teens choose to keep their smoking a secret, which usually does not last long if parents are keeping a close watch. For the teens reading this book, once you have communicated with your parents it is important to respect their wishes the best you can.

Here is an example of not being respectful: I know a young person who would sometimes smoke in her bedroom and blow the smoke out an open window. Unfortunately, she would stink up the whole house. Her mother was clear: "Do not smoke in the house!" And yet she would smoke in her room anyway. Is this a smart pot smoker? How do you think her (single) mother, raising her and two younger brothers, felt about it?

Remember, it is illegal for anyone under the age of twenty-one to smoke or possess pot. Period. Even if your state is *cool* about pot and has decriminalized it or made it legal for medical use, or even made it legal for people over twenty-one, this is not a green light for you to smoke whenever and wherever you want. Smart teens are discreet.

Teens who choose to smoke pot and also achieve success at home and school have some common traits: they do not smoke before or at school, they get their school work done on time and maintain good grades, they have a circle of friends with whom they share other interests besides pot. They are, more than less, honest with themselves and others. They trust their parents are not extreme and are people that with whom they can talk about almost anything.

REFLECTION: How much pot did you buy the first time? How long did it last?

Be discreet.

THE DRAMA

SECRETS AND LIES

Smoking pot, at least in the beginning, usually means hiding it from adults, especially parents. Some adults are able to communicate non-judgmentally, rather than judge or condemn. The job of a parent is to say no when needed. Some parents are incredibly strict and extreme. Some parents seem to not care or are not around; some even smoke with their kids. Most parents are somewhere in the middle.

Let's say your family is somewhere in the middle of extreme and lenient, which means there are some secrets, manipulation, and lies, and some honesty, responsibility, and accountability. Parents (or a single parent), if they are good communicators and observers, know teens may try pot, and have a right to voice their opinion while not screaming about the subject. (Does anyone really listen while being screamed at?) Balanced parents are not overly intrusive, nor are they too easygoing. Skillful parents will let you know how they feel yet offer you their trust until you give them a reason not to. The ideal parents have the right balance of give and take, firmness and gentleness. Your parent's job is tough and they will not always do what you want. They are not always going to be your best friend. Their "job" is to speak up and keep the peace. Absolutely, they should listen to your side of the story. And hopefully you feel heard. They should also set the rules. Ideally, parents are trusted advisors. This means offering a philosophy of life that encompasses honest values, respect, and kindness toward yourself and others.

Ultimately, your parents have the final say regarding your comings and goings. They are the *boss*. Hopefully you can be responsible, sincere, and honest with them, and they will do the same for you, creating a *win-win* relationship. Win-win means even though your parents are in charge, you know they are doing a good job taking care of you. And you are doing a good job taking care of yourself.

Whatever your relationship is with your parents, do your best to be responsible. For example, come home when you say you will, do well in school, and keep in touch when you are out and about. This is not that difficult, and it will make your life much more pleasant. If possible, let your parents know what you need, and ask about what they need.

REFLECTION: What are some of your secrets and lies?

Busted.

I HATE YOU

Because you are a teen—still getting to know your strengths and weaknesses, as well as dealing with changing hormones—there is a good chance you will, at some point, get upset and do or say things that you regret. That is normal. You may have even blurted out an "I hate you!" once or twice. Maybe you mean it, maybe you don't. Adults say mean things they regret also (and sometimes they act like adolescents). But if you are too easily carried away by your emotions, it may feel like you are never in control. And feeling out of control may lead to increased anxiety or increased drug use. Some people smoke pot because they are feeling angry or sad (often for good reasons). There are healthy ways to deal with your emotions, and one of the best is to recognize your feelings and talk about them with someone you trust.

Whatever strong emotions you may feel toward you parents, whether you feel your parents are unfair or everything you do is wrong—or whatever the feeling—it is important to let them know what is on your mind. They may not want to hear it, but it is best to say it anyway. If possible, let them know what you need with a calm voice. At least try to keep a peaceful manner as you come and go. That means that if they want to talk, do your best to listen. Perhaps ask them, "What do you need me to do for you to trust me?" And always do your best to keep calm.

If you are feeling lost, consider this: You are not lost. You are here. In this moment, give yourself a little space and time to sit still and breathe without thinking. Focus on your breath. Imagine exhaling your thoughts and take a little vacation from your worries. After a little while you may notice you can see more clearly. This is also known as a "mindfulness meditation" which is an excellent way to reduce stress.

Everything changes.

REFLECTION: How often, if ever, do you get upset with your parents? Why?

Sometimes it feels like no one understands.

COMMUNICATION

How you express yourself, with words, tone, body language, and even silence, is your communication style. Some styles are: assertive, passive, insecure, dramatic, truthful, agreeable, humble, aggressive, loud, quiet, angry, manipulative, pleasing—and many combinations thereof, to name a few. In fact, your tone of voice and body language reveal more information than do your words. Did you know you speak without words?

Most parents confront their teens once they find out they are smoking pot—some more skillfully than others. Skillful parents will guide and let you find your way, if they trust you. Communication between parents and adolescents can be awkward and resentment can be a problem if an issue goes too long without being voiced. Some parents will belittle and shame you when they find out you smoke pot. Other parents will let you know how they feel, set realistic boundaries, and try to keep you safe. It is good to always keep in mind that your parents have a right to challenge and talk to you. That is their job, though you may not like it! So communication is inevitable and often helpful.

I encourage families to talk about what makes them upset and work respectfully with one another to create resolutions, seeing and acknowledging each other's opinion. This is also called collaboration.

If your parents are unable to communicate with you, for whatever reason, then communicate with another trusted adult or friend.

REFLECTION: What is your communication style with your parents?

Some parents know how to communicate...some don't.

PARENT(S)

Why do you think your parents worry about you smoking pot?

Try to see through their eyes. Is it because they care about you and want you to be safe? Do they worry you will do something stupid and get hurt? Do your parents even know you smoke? Or are they never around and don't seem to care? There are many parenting styles. Usually, parents just want what they believe is the best for you.

Parents pass on to you not only genetics that affects your potential for long life or illness, but they also pass on to you their temperament, opinions, habits, moods, and manners. And all this is passed on by behavior—how they act. It has little to do with words and more with tone and body language.

Hopefully, your parents are responsible and mellow, with a minimum of anger and drama in the house, and all those things you see your parents do, say, or not say, you feel pretty good about. Stable families with mutual respect, clear rules, and greater trust, spend quality time together, and they do better than families that have no trust or clear rules.

Effective parents teach by example how to manage emotions, be safe, and take responsibility. Everyone wants parents who are cool, listening with both ears and eyes. To build confidence and not shame, skillful parents know when to remain silent, let go, and just watch, as well as when to speak up and say no.

Some parents are stuck in their own personal drama or anger that has nothing to do with you. You may even feel your parents' problems are all your fault, but that is not the case. Your parents are human and have their own unique problems and fears.

Whether your family system is healthy or not, you—the you who questions and dreams in the night, the you who is confused and testing the world, experimenting—you are not only a product of your parents, you are unique. And one day, you will be on your own to define your world as you wish.

REFLECTION: What do you wish your parent(s) would do differently?

With any luck, your parents are good communicators.

THE GOOD-ENOUGH PARENT

The *good-enough* parent is the ideal. The good-enough parent walks the middle ground between trust and fear, punishment and reward, freedom and discipline. They know how to say "I'm sorry," if needed. In contrast, what is not healthy, for example, is when parents get drunk, display a lot of intense emotion, or are screaming, yelling, name-calling, manipulating, lying, or showing disrespect toward or around you. Sadly, some teens are parenting their parents.

No one is perfect, and this is not a parent bash. The good-enough parent is not perfect, but one thing is for sure, there is trust that goes both ways—with a good-enough parent (as often as possible) there is deep listening, validation, and mindful speech. There is balanced mix of patience and action. The good-enough parent knows how to keep an eye on you, be present in your life, and give you directions when needed. The good-enough parent also knows how and when to give you space, when to say yes and when to say no, because they are...good-enough. Most importantly, the good-enough parent is patient and mindful with themselves if they are having a difficult day. There is no one thing a parent can do to be good-enough. Being good-enough is a continuum of trial and error.

Regarding your smoking pot, good-enough parents need something from you—to stay out of trouble with school or the police—and to be smart about pot! They need to trust you to be good-enough. It goes both ways. Good-enough parents show a balance between listening deeply, going with the flow, and taking charge and setting limits. *Good-enough* teens who smoke pot occasionally will do well in school and stay out of trouble—they know how to have fun, get things done, and respect their parents. How do teens who smoke pot stay out of trouble? Many are discreet and only smoke when it is safe. Practicing harm reduction begins with common sense.

A friend of mine, who is a local policeman, and his wife, knew their seventeen-year-old son was around pot and alcohol at parties. The boy was honest with his parents. His parents, being laid-back and relaxed, yet strict when needed, gave their son room to be himself, and they did not stop him from going to parties. This was between ages sixteen to eighteen. His school grades were As and Bs with a few Cs. Sometimes, the boy came home from parties after smoking pot or even drinking a little, and the parents knew it. But, the boy was doing well at home, school, and with friends, so his parents gave his some room to experiment. They knew when to speak and when to let go. The boy went on to college and is now a successful lawyer.

REFLECTION: Can you describe your perfect mom or dad?

Remember to say "I love you."

EXTREME PARENTS

Extreme parenting is different from good enough, because it crosses the line of emotional or physical safety. For a teen with extreme parents, life can be downright horrible. There are many variations of this, but some examples of extremes are:

- Emotional Abuse (manipulation, extreme disrespect, control, or drama, etc.)
- Physical abuse (any violence that bruises your body, etc.)
- Verbal abuse (putting you down with words, calling you names, etc.)
- Alcohol abuse or drug abuse (a parent who gets visibly drunk nightly is alcoholic, one or two drinks a night is okay…)

If you have extreme parents, even if your family is wrapped in a pretty house on a pretty street, their extreme behavior around you usually causes intense worry and anxiety. An extreme parental situation will also say a lot about why you might be smoking pot.

Most parents are not extreme; they show some combination of kindness, discipline, and respect. However, if you feel unsafe, there are some effective ways to deal with extreme parents. First, depending how extreme your parents are, if possible, try talking with them about your concerns. Trust your gut. If it is too emotionally dangerous to speak to your parents, talk about your feelings to an adult you trust, perhaps a school counselor, teacher, or someone outside of the home. Sometimes, all you can do is try and stay clear of the drama in your family and do your best to ask for help elsewhere. Stay with a trusted friend, if necessary. Extreme parents are among the most difficult challenges for teens.

Keep in mind that you are not helplessly caught by your circumstances—not now, not ever. You have the ability to choose your words, thoughts, and actions. Ask for help if you need it.

REFLECTION: How do you define an extreme parent?

You cannot control other people or events,
but you can control your response.

BOUNDARIES

Boundaries are not only invisible lines that mark the limits of an area, like boundaries between countries or property, boundaries are also the things you say or do that keep you emotionally safe. Parents need to have healthy boundaries with their teens, and teens need healthy boundaries with themselves and others. It is not a healthy boundary, for example, if a parent constantly walks into their teen's room without knocking. What does that teach? Is that parent respecting privacy?

Choosing to not smoke pot in school is an example of choosing a good boundary. That choice keeps you safe from being expelled, developing a bad reputation, or being grounded at home. Some teens like to take more risks than others. If you smoke pot, there are many important boundaries to not cross, and things you must simply not do. Do you think partying until you pass out is a good personal boundary?

What are some smart boundaries?

- Keep your personal business private, only sharing among close friends.
- Be aware of the words, photos, or emotions that you show in public (including the Internet). Think before you speak; hold back, if necessary.

- Let your parents know what you need and ask for their trust.
- Be trustworthy.
- Get to know yourself—what works for you and what works against you.
- Know which actions keep you safe and which are dangerous.
- Be mindful of your speech, remembering words can be used to hurt or help.

Good boundaries keep you safe.

REFLECTION: What are some of your most important boundaries?

Know your limits.

POT-SMOKING PARENTS

Many adults who currently smoke pot also have teens who smoke pot. In that situation, pot smoking parents have a responsibility to maintain good boundaries with their teens—like not smoking pot with them, for example, and keeping it private.

I know some parents who smoke pot around their teens or even with them. I have one friend who buys pot for his teenage son, because he wants to protect his son from having to buy it himself from "some loser." In my opinion, these are examples of poor parenting boundaries. I also know some parents who ask their teenage children to get them pot, which is also not cool. That is a perfect example of poor boundary maintenance and crosses the line into unsafe.

Down the road, when a teen is out of the house and at college or successful in a job and on their own, maybe then a pot smoking family might sit down together and 'roll one up,' if that feels right. I know some parents who have smoked with their adult children (who are twenty-one years or older and have a job), and I think that is more acceptable. Until then, parents who smoke pot should keep it private. Don't you agree? If your parents ask you to smoke pot with them, why not think twice? You should feel free to say, "No, thanks. I'm not comfortable with that."

REFLECTION: Do you think it is okay for teens to smoke with their parents?

Uncomfortable.

SAFE

You have one of three choices with pot:

1. Don't smoke.
2. Smoke and be stupid.
3. Smoke and be smart.

Being smart also means being as safe as possible. Being safe about pot means making good choices concerning smoking and adjusting your attitude day-to-day, even moment-to-moment.

Some of the biggest *unsafe* mistakes teens make are:

1. Smoking with the wrong group—some people are simply a bad influence because they are into hard drugs and excess drinking, or they are potentially violent.
2. Smoking too much or too often and messing up school and/or homelife (poor choices, poor grades, etc.).
3. Smoking at the wrong time and place—which can draw the attention of the authorities or harm yourself and others. For example, you should *not* smoke and drive.

These biggest mistakes can lead to numerous smaller problems as well—and the damage from some, such as smoking and driving, can potentially never be undone. One golden teen rule is: never get totally wasted—always stop before you lose all control and soundness of judgment.

REFLECTION: Do you feel safe when you are smoking pot?

The opposite of smart.

SCHOOL

Someone once told me, "To change the world, you need to get into the world." Generally, (not always) graduating from school is an excellent way to get into the world. Getting into the world means playing by the rules and dealing with responsibility. I was an average student. In middle and high school, I earned mostly A's, B's, and C's with the occasional D in my classes. However, I could write and went on to excel at an excellent university, which I loved. College was actually easier than high school, because I enjoyed the work so much. It is not that hard to get As and Bs when you simply enjoy what you are doing. Sure, it takes some hard work. But did you know showing up and doing your work with a decent attitude is 90 percent of success in life.

It is important to do your best with school and homework, graduate from high school, and consider going on to college or vocational school.

If for any reason smoking pot is getting in the way of school, your grades—or, in the worst case, graduation—then please take a break from smoking pot until the problem is resolved.

Successful teens may sometimes smoke pot, but they have good study habits, like not smoking before school, taking good notes in class, and turning in homework on time.

REFLECTION: What is the pot situation at your school? Do many people smoke?

Golden rule, don't smoke at school.

COLLEGE

The same guidelines that apply to high school apply to smoking pot at college, as well. If you go away to college, there will be no one looking after you, telling you when to come home or where to go. You are on your own. You are free! But freedom requires right action. So being smart about your free time is even more important than when you were in high school.

If you choose not to go to a four-year college, then please consider an associate degree or a certification in a skills program at a community college or a vocational school. College is not for everyone. Careers such as electrician, IT technician, web designer, office manager, hairdresser, massage therapist, medical assistant, paralegal, mechanic, among others, offer satisfying work and pay well. Besides, graduating from vocational training or a two-year college is a great way to build character and meet people. Finding an interest you are passionate about makes studying much easier.

REFLECTION: What is your dream job?

"Later dude!" is always an option.

KNOWING YOURSELF

TOO MUCH

How do you know if you are smoking too much pot for your own good?

Smoking too much pot will mean that you have begun going down the *wrong* road. If you don't know you have a problem, others around you may tell you, but you should always be on the lookout so you can catch it before it gets too serious. What are problem pot smokers doing? They are smoking daily, skipping school, getting poor grades, making poor decisions, acting out, perhaps fighting, becoming angry or depressed—all signs that you have crossed the line of what's good for you.

There are limits, unique to your body, determining how much marijuana is enough for you to feel good, and how much will cause harm. As a teenager, one of your jobs is figuring out what is too much for you, whether it is studying, eating, arguing, or doing things you should not be doing. How much is enough? Remember, it can take up to fifteen minutes to feel the full effect of smoking pot. What happens to you during and after smoking? Are you feeling good? If not, why even bother smoking pot? You are in charge of you.

While you may not overdose, you can certainly smoke so much pot that it gets in the way of your success in life. Back off if you need to. If you find smoking pot interferes with the smallest of daily expectations, like going to school, fulfilling your potential, and maintaining positive relationships with family and friends, it is time to stop smoking.

It is okay to say, "No thanks, I'm good" if you don't want any more.

REFLECTION: Have you ever smoked too much pot? What was that like?

Too much is too much.

HEALTH

Just because pot is a "natural plant" does not mean it is harmless. In fact, science knows pot is dangerous under certain conditions. For example, if you have a preexisting mental illness, an addictive personality, or you drink and use harder drugs, marijuana can make matters much worse. A twenty-three-year-old man died unexpectedly after smoking marijuana. Later, they discovered he had a heart condition. Lesson: people with vulnerable hearts should not smoke pot.

As more teens smoke marijuana, concerns will arise over the effects smoking has on teen development. As noted earlier, your brain is developing into your twenties and science does not fully understand how smoking will affect your long-term development, but initial research finds that excessive pot smoking changes the shape of certain areas of the teenage brain. What science does not know is how this compares to other activities that change the "shape" of the brain, like whether excessively playing violent video games has long-term implications. What we do know is that your teen brain is still forming and smoking marijuana effects your motivation. Science does not know for sure if or how teen pot smoking affects adult life.

An amazing study at the University of California has shown *low to moderate* smoking of pot does not cause lung cancer.

However, if you add cigarettes to smoking pot, the risk of getting lung cancer was present. The lesson, quit smoking cigarettes or vaping. If you don't know already, you do now: Vaping is highly addictive. If you vape consider cutting down.

What else might happen if you smoke a lot of pot over many years? Cough. Over time, there is an increased incidence of wheezing, coughing, and bronchitis for heavy pot smokers. If you smoke too much, for too long, you will likely cough. Studies also showed that if the study subjects stopped smoking pot, the breathing difficulties often went away.

Emotionally speaking, smoking pot may lead to some health concerns. Research has shown that smoking pot can increase emotional problems in some people, especially people with preexisting mental illnesses like schizophrenia. There have also been links to increased depression in some chronic users. What science does not understand is how many teens are already struggling with depression or other mental illnesses, like anxiety or phobias, before they start smoking marijuana.

If you or anyone in your family has ever had severe mental illness, it may be best to stay away from pot.

REFLECTION: How does smoking pot effect your health—mental, physical, and emotional?

Maybe pot's not for you.

ADDICTION

While marijuana is not *physically* addicting, you can become *emotionally* addicted to it.

Psychological or emotional addiction is different from physical addiction. If, after habitual use, you stop taking something like heroin, cocaine, nicotine, or oxycodone, your body will go through physical withdrawal, because you have become physically addicted. It is an awful feeling to come off an opiate addiction, and your body will temporarily get very sick when you stop. That is why many people go to a rehabilitation clinic to get off hard drugs. Marijuana is generally not like that. However, if you have other psychological problems, pot may land you in rehab. There are teens who have addictive personalities and are more prone to excessiveness and addiction than others.

Any kind of addiction is not good. Once addicted, you have lost control, and the drug is using you. Too much of anything indicates you have insufficient impulse control. The problem may occur before you realize you have a problem, which means others may notice it before you do.

Here is a test to see if you have a pot problem: if you are a regular smoker, see if you can stop for one month. Stopping cold turkey might make you feel cranky, angry, sad, or needy; your mind may crave it, and you *feel* like you need it. But if you stop smoking pot you will not get physically sick, as you would when coming off opiates. Can you do it? If you find it impossible to stop, you have a problem.

Like a long-distance runner, if you set your pace too fast at the beginning of the race, you will burn out before the end; it's the same with smoking pot. Be mindful not to smoke too frequently because frequent use contributes to the development of addiction. Make an effort not to smoke every day. Being a teen is hard enough. Having marijuana problems on top of that is something you do not need.

Addiction creeps up on anyone who does anything too much, and before you know it, you are stuck or sick. Being smart about smoking pot now means not having to get unstuck later. If you think you have a problem smoking pot, communicate—try talking to a friend or a trusted adult. You can also check out some of the resources on our website.

You will be surprised to know there are many confidential options for help.

REFLECTION: Do you think pot is addictive? Why?

Can you turn down a pot for a month?

POT VS. ALCOHOL

According to a survey conducted by the National Institutes of Health: National Institute on Drug Abuse, alcohol consumption among teens has declined steadily since 2007, while marijuana use has increased. This indicates pot is becoming more popular among young people. Nonetheless, alcohol abuse by teens remains far too common and far more dangerous and destructive than marijuana abuse. And if you combine the two, then you are asking for trouble.

Alcohol abuse and drinking until you're wasted are directly linked to the loss of fine motor control and basic judgment, which can lead to things like fatal car accidents, a greater propensity for violent confrontation, unprotected sex, and serious physical and mental deterioration over the long term. The fact is, teens are far more likely to see parents drink to excess, or drink and drive, than smoke pot to excess leading to a catastrophic accident.

Marijuana offers a different set of problems, and we are learning more about it every day in terms of the developing teenage brain. No doubt, there will be many studies in the years ahead on the subject of marijuana and teen development. So stay tuned. In the meantime, if you are going to drink to excess it may prove fatal. We generally do not see the mental and physical devastation with marijuana use that we see with alcohol abuse.

Pot is not harmless. While no healthy person whom I know of has died from an overdose of marijuana, many people have gotten sick, smoked too much for their own good, or failed out of school because of poor choices. However, with marijuana we generally do not see the mental and physical devastation that we see with alcohol abuse. Families are destroyed, jobs lost, and marriages crumble, all because of alcohol.

So do yourself a favor, try skipping alcohol the next time it is offered. And don't smoke pot to excess.

REFLECTION: Which drug do you think is more dangerous—alcohol or pot? Why?

Being smart with pot means being smarter with alcohol.

POLICE

Pot is definitely not accepted by everyone. Sometimes a person smoking pot will cross paths with a police officer for one reason or another, like smoking in the wrong place at the wrong time or getting pulled over and the police smell it.

Even though marijuana has been decriminalized for adults in several states, it remains illegal for teens in every state in the United States. As a teen, you are taking a legal risk just by possessing pot or related paraphernalia, not to mention smoking it. Some states are much stricter than others; however, I imagine police probably do not want to ruin the lives of a teenager with an arrest record for marijuana possession. Of course, if you are selling pot, that is another story and may land you a criminal record.

If you are stopped by an officer (or if an officer enters your home) be polite and honest. Regarding small amounts of marijuana—and depending on the city or state you live in—some police officers will give you a warning, call your parents, and/or send you on your way. Other officers will give you a hard time and can issue what is called a minor in possession (MIP) or other such charge. In any scenario with the police, take it seriously, because it may affect your future.

Know your rights. If arrested, you do not need to volunteer information, and you can remain silent until you get a lawyer or your guardian is contacted. However, if you are stopped by police, always speak respectfully and remain calm.

REFLECTION: Have you ever had an encounter with the police regarding pot? What happened?

Uh-oh.

STRESS

The life of a teenager is stressful. Many teens smoke pot to alleviate stress. Academic expectations, social pressures, school, and homelife can add up to a lot of stress.

Even the most successful people in the world have stress. You can do well in school, your parents might be cool, your friends are good, and you have all the stuff that makes life worthwhile—that does not mean that you won't have any stress. Shit happens even to the most fortunate people. People lose tempers and say things they don't mean. Friends and parents can disappoint us; some parents are a mess, and the kids are affected by it. Some teens have more stress than others. Some things you can control, some things you can't. The point is, stress is a part of life, and if you smoke pot, it is not the answer to your problems.

The American Psychological Association's Stress in America Survey examined the stress habits of one thousand teens. Teen stressors included homework, grades, work, friendships, and family relations. More than 30 percent of teens reported that stress caused them to lose sleep and feel sad and depressed, and 25 percent said stress made them skip meals. The survey also found teen girls are more stressed than teen boys.

Stress is not just what happens to you, but also how you react to it. How one reacts depends on how one sees something. For example, while some teens might see their parents getting divorced as horrible, some might see it as sad but necessary, because they know their parents will do better apart than they would together. Everyone gets stressed; that is normal. How you see that stress, however, is a choice. You can actually choose (with practice) what thoughts to have, what thoughts to let go, and how to think about things.

Good communication, exercise and sports, prayer, meditation, yoga, and eating well are options for reducing stress. If you are extremely unhappy because of your stress (for whatever reason) or feel awful most of the time, then it is time to ask for help. You can always talk to a counselor or call a crisis line.

REFLECTION: What stresses you out the most? How do you cope with it?

How you respond to stress is a choice.

IS POT MEDICINE?

Some people say marijuana is a medicinal plant or an herbal medicine. And they think because it is a plant, it is harmless. Did you know certain herbs, seeds, or berries can kill you? The way I see it, yes, pot is a plant, but it is also a drug with chemicals that will change your mood.

Depending on your condition, pot also relieves physical and mental pain, and for certain diseases, it brings relief.

Question is, if pot is a kind of medicine, what is the ailment? Multiple sclerosis, cancer, HIV, glaucoma, chronic pain, anxiety? We know pot can significantly reduce discomfort for various illnesses and reduce the side effects of certain cancer treatments.

Teens rarely think about why they smoke pot. Maybe there is something wrong in your family, or you don't feel good about yourself, and smoking takes away that emotional pain. Maybe you are bored, stressed, or anxious. You may smoke for no other reason than you like it—it is fun and relaxing, and it can make you feel more creative. To know yourself is to know your motivations.

REFLECTION: Why do you smoke pot?

Pot helps his MS

THE STATE OF MODERN HERB

Today's pot is not yesterday's. There are several levels of potency, from *commercial grade* to *medical grade*. The strongest pot is over 30% THC. Commercial pot in the United States primarily comes from Mexico and other Latin American countries. Medical-grade pot is generally grown and controlled in the United States for adult consumption and is becoming a big business, with the most exotic and expensive grades being genetically modified to produce a certain feeling after smoking. The level of THC in pot varies based on the strain or type of pot you smoke, with the commercial grade being weaker than the medical. Sativa and Indica are the two main types of marijuana, and there are dozens of variations and hybrids. Some strains of pot will wake you up, and some are deeply relaxing.

As we saw earlier, THC levels in pot are on the rise, and the strongest pot is up to 27 percent THC (according to the University of Mississippi Monitoring Project). Compare this to the average 3 percent of the seventies.

One thing is for sure—marijuana today is stronger than ever before. You do not need to smoke very much to get high.

REFLECTION: Have you ever felt like you smoked too much pot?

Strong stuff.

POLITICS

As pot becomes more available for adults as certain states decriminalize it, there is a concern that teens will get the wrong message. Is it true that, the more that adults are cool with smoking pot, the more teens will think they can smoke it without a problem? Perhaps. The verdict is clear about one thing—too much of anything, over time, will harm you.

Marijuana for adults is a growing multibillion-dollar industry. And "Weed, Inc." will keep on growing. So far, the US federal authorities are leaving the states alone. Whether you agree or disagree, America's relationship with marijuana is changing toward tolerance and acceptance among adults, even as I write these words.

Present-day pot politics are in flux, for adults. However, if up to two million teens are going to smoke pot on any given day, respectful communication on the subject with parents is a good idea.

Time will tell if teens who smoke marijuana will manage their personal pot consumption skillfully.

REFLECTION: Do you think people should be allowed to smoke pot at age 18-19, like in Canada? Why?

Times are changing.

THE NEXT LEVEL

SUCCESS

Success is defined differently at different stages of our life. Success for you, as a teen, might be feeling good about yourself, having parents you can talk to who treat you with love and respect, always doing your personal best, having good friends, treating your friends and yourself with love and respect, not doing anything to harm yourself or others, getting good grades in school, dealing with your parents and other adults as politely as possible, having a decent part-time job, and someday getting ready to go to college or some kind of vocational training. You get the idea.

Success for an adult might be a loving relationship, enjoyable job, good health, travel, abundant money, rewarding work, dear friends, and having healthy, successful children.

There is also as many variations as there are people on the planet: each person ultimately defines what success means to them by deciding what matters to them most in life.

One way to discover your strengths is to search out what you like, love, and are good at. This means trying out different subjects, activities, or ideas, as well as being willing to take reasonable risks. The more you experience success, the more confident you will become.

REFLECTION: What is your personal definition of success for yourself—today, and in five years?

Everyone has their own personal definition of success.

CREATIVITY

Some artistic people feel that smoking pot helps their creative process.

Artists, composers, poets, philosophers, and writers through the centuries are among the many who have indulged in the occasional smoking of pot (or other intoxicants) to free up their creative juices. However, this may not lead to the healthiest of lifestyles and is not for everyone. There is a time and place for creativity.

In my experience as a performer, the creative state is God-given and will reveal itself without pot. Inspiration will be revealed at a moment's notice, and you either pay attention to it or not. Once inspired, then the hard work begins to make a dream come true.

While creativity is a source of progress, each of us must find a personal balance between being creative and being practical. Not everyone has a creative personality, yet everyone can cultivate and harness creative energy. Don't ever be afraid to think differently or follow your creative dreams. Creativity may not be practical, but it is honest.

The psychologist Carl Jung understood the creative forces of a person. He said:

The secret of artistic creation and of the effectiveness of art is to be found in a return to the state of *participation mystique.*

The "participation mystique" is a level of creativity where the individual (you) disappears, and all of humanity participates and is touched. The artist captures something bigger than herself, and it's all you can do to get out of the way, listen deeply, and work hard to create a single finished product.

REFLECTION: Do you feel creative when you smoke pot? What happens?

Big dreams and hard work can change the world.

A JOB-JOB

Many hard workers have been known to smoke pot occasionally.

Andrew Carnegie once said, "Anything in life worth having is worth working for." So if you are going to live successfully, with rewards and fulfillment, and make good money, you need a good job.

Hopefully, you are open to working part time, beginning around the age of fifteen or sixteen, if possible. There are lots of jobs for teens that pay minimum wage, and some may even be enjoyable. It is true that some teens do not need to work. I think that is all the more reason to work. Why not earn your own money and build independence?

In the future, you will seek a job that suits your personality and personal abilities (a combination of what interests you and what you're capable of doing). For now, though, when you're ready, you just need a "job-job"—something that is not too bad—in order to make money. If you truly enjoy your part-time job, all the better. Keep in mind, these are temporary jobs to cover your expenses, taken while on your way to college or technical school.

Always strive to make money doing what you enjoy. Taking a few odd jobs along the way can help build independence and allow you to pay for the things you want.

REFLECTION: Do you think teens should have a part time job?

Some after school jobs may even be...enjoyable.

LOVE

You may ask what love has to do with smoking marijuana and harm reduction.

One reason teens may smoke pot is to cover up the emotional pain they are experiencing.

From an early age, if you rarely receive or experience love, or receive love in a manipulative, destructive, confusing manner, it will be hard to love and trust other people. You may excel in your work or school, but trusting others and maintaining healthy social skills may be challenging.

Love comes in different packages. There is love in the grand sense…love of life, humanity, God, hope, goodwill for all, love of creating a work of art, love of doing what you are good at, helping others, etc. There is love of family, friends, pets. There is romantic love of a girlfriend or boyfriend. There is love of nature. There is spiritual love. The list goes on. Each expression of love has a different voice and expectation.

A day comes for all of us when we feel a little or a lot alone, and all the smarts in the world will not take that lonely feeling away. But love, friends, and family, sure help.

Everything will change. Nothing stays the same. If you are having a hard time with something, ask for help, or give yourself time to figure things out.

REFLECTION: Why do you think you are smoking pot?

It's hard to give love if you have never received love.

THE TRUE YOU

In the quiet of your mind, there is a wise part that knows, or perhaps senses, what is right and what is wrong, what is too much, and what is too little. Some people call it "our true Self." It has its own little voice and can talk you through almost any challenge.

Though you are still discovering your strengths and weaknesses, you always have access to this wise place in your Self. Lasting happiness comes from within. There is no external thing that brings deep contentment. External things can feel fabulous for a while, but it does not last.

Lasting happiness is a state of mind and grace that no one can take away. Happiness, or being content with what you have, is a dance of effort and letting go. The effort is the awareness—working through life's challenges and obstacles. The letting go, sometimes moment-to-moment, yields the reward and gives you space to see clearly what is real and what is an illusion. And in between "effort and letting go" is a place where you spend a lot of time growing up, discovering, and moving from adolescence to adulthood.

In order to be smart about any "bad" habits you may have, you need to know yourself and ask good questions that actually protect you in the long run from the potential of letting that "bad" habit get in the way of your success. If you smoke pot or not, if you are a good kid or a "problem" kid, get to know the wise self within, who is always looking after your highest good.

REFLECTION: When are you most happy?

When in doubt, listen to your inner voice.

JUST ONE PUFF

If you do not smoke marijuana, I hope this book has offered you some helpful considerations and insights about the subject, and that whatever decision you make, you will be safe and successful.

If you do smoke pot, here is the challenge: Why not take just one puff?

You do not need more than one puff to get high.

You will find, especially with today's potent pot, you need no more than one puff to feel good. It is true that human beings, all of us, often want more of what we like than is necessary or good for us. However, the message of harm reduction in this book boils down to making smart choices and choosing smart actions.

The smart pot smoker knows how often he or she should smoke pot. The smart pot smoker may even take a pot break, for a few weeks or months, or longer, just to make sure they are not addicted. Sure, if you are smoking pot, you may want more than one puff. But that does not mean that you have to take it.

REFLECTION: Can you take just one puff when you smoke pot?

One puff is enough.

WORDS, WORDS, WORDS

Action is the language that defines humanity. Words mean little without action.

Now that you have read this little book, it is time to utilize the ideas for yourself. Apply some of the ideas for harm reduction by putting them into action. You have to walk your own path, and no book can walk it for you, but books can help; they are essential for personal growth. Just as lifting weights and exercise can build your muscles and bones, books can strengthen your understanding and point you in the right direction.

If you do decide to smoke pot, no matter what you read or hear, you will figure out how to smoke as you go along. By *how*, I mean what is right for you—how often, when, and where. You will have lots of chances to practice the ideas in this book and make mistakes.

There is no need to always know the right answers or even know what or why you do what you do. But there is a need (for all of us) to be responsible and smart about the *not knowing*.

REFLECTION: Aren't we are all hypocrites one way or another? Why do you suppose that is?

Check this out.

STRENGTH IS ALSO
VULNERABILITY

Smoking pot occasionally does not take away the hard work, deep caring, success, failures, and accomplishments of life that make up the diversity that keeps you fresh and alive. More important than any drug is caring for your well-being and the well-being of others. That takes time, years; don't worry about getting there. The journey is often the reward.

I am not sure who wrote the quote below, but I like it. It is about being able to feel good about yourself. Behind every smart pot smoker, every person who cares about working for balance in life, is a person who is living life fearlessly...

> Look at yourself and into yourself without shying away from what you might find there. Once you get beyond being embarrassed and worried about knowing yourself, you come to the real nature of your heart. You find that it is soft, tender, and open. Experiencing the basic goodness of our lives makes us feel that the world is not a threat.

The lesson: allow yourself to be vulnerable sometimes, without any self-judgment.

REFLECTION: What do you like about you? What is good?

It takes courage to be vulnerable.

REINVENT YOURSELF

O ur country is an optimistic nation that believes that all people have the right to reinvent themselves for the better, no matter what mistakes they make. Reinvent means to change how the world sees you and how you see yourself. This is an acknowledgment that you live in a place where you can be yourself, make mistakes, figure things out, and learn to do things differently. Other countries are not so free.

They say it takes twenty-one days of a new action to change a habit. Smoking pot easily becomes a habit. *As I said earlier, this book is not meant to promote or discourage the smoking of marijuana.* It is a book for harm reduction and success. Harm reduction and success for a teenage pot smoker means constantly being willing to admit mistakes, make adjustments, and act differently, as needed. That willingness to act differently for your own good is called reinventing yourself. Every day can be a *do-over.*

REFLECTION: Is there something you would like to change about yourself?

Never be afraid to reinvent yourself.

GOOD-BYE

One thing you can count on in life is that nothing will stay the same, which is a good reason to reread the book every once in a while. As you grow and change, rereading the book will offer new meanings. Strange how that works. Same words, different insight, over time. In the end, I hope you nurture at least one message: if you choose to smoke pot you are fully capable of making *smart* choices and doing your personal best. It is about using your willpower and character for the greater good, including your own.

Principles are what keep us from failing. They are both guidelines and beliefs. In contrast, the problem marijuana smoker is someone who has lost control of certain principles, whose willpower wanes—and maybe for only a few reasons, like stress, trauma, genetics, mild or serious mental illness, or lack of maturity.

I once heard a teacher say, "As you get older, one of two things will happen. You will grow softer or harder."

Growing softer is being flexible, letting go, accepting life in its light, joy, and sorrow, rolling with the disappointments, failures, and the unexpected, cultivating joy and love, taking responsibility, speaking up when needed, and following up your beliefs with actions. Growing harder is becoming angry and rigid, resisting change, fighting people and life, holding on to resentments, having to be right all the time, hating, blaming others, feeling entitled. The lesson? How you handle this moment determines the next. In the end, harm reduction is a way of life: moment-to-moment choices that shape us over time, visibly and invisibly for the better.

And that brings us to good-bye. Let me know online how things go at www.thecannabiscraze.com.

Make room and enjoy the mystery and the unknown. Life is a wonderful journey. And if you happen to take the "road less traveled," you may find it makes all the difference.

Bon voyage, good journey, pot or no pot.

ABOUT THE AUTHOR

Marc was born in Detroit, Michigan. At various points in his teens he was encouraged to explore his creative side, including writing, dance, and theatre. Eventually he went off to college to study theatre. Theatre led to a dance class which led to a career as a professional modern dancer in Europe and New York City. In the early nineties Marc reinvented himself (you cannot dance forever) by completing a masters in counseling psychology and developing a hip-hop dance-based counseling program for at-risk youth, titled the Berkshire Project. (www.berkshireproject.org). Marc currently works as a consultant and licensed mental health counselor in Lenox, Massachusetts.

ABOUT THE ILLUSTRATOR

Earl Cavanah is a native Californian with a BFA in advertising design. During his thirty years as an art director and creative director on Madison Avenue, Earl has garnered over 150 awards, including two Gold Lions at the Cannes Film Festival for his work on television commercials. After drawing thousands of story boards, this is Earl's first book for young adults. Earl currently works as a creative consultant in Westchester County, NY.

CPSIA information can be obtained
at www.ICGtesting.com
Printed in the USA
LVHW071657150519

617945LV00041B/488/P